Great Gardens in Small Spaces

California Havens

GREAT GARDENS IN SMALL SPACES

CALIFORNIA HAVENS

PHOTOGRAPHY MELBA LEVICK

TEXT KAREN DARDICK

RIZZOLI
NEW YORK

First published in the United States of America in 2003 by
RIZZOLI INTERNATIONAL PUBLICATIONS, INC.
300 Park Avenue South, New York, NY 10010
www.rizzoliusa.com

ISBN: 0-8478-2538-8
LCCN: 2003100743

Front cover: "Outdoor Rooms," Scott Shrader's Garden (p. 220)
Back cover: A Profusion of Color, Sunny and Susan Estrada's Garden (p. 226)
Pages 1 and 8: A Tropical Scene, Marian Ross' Garden (p. 94)
Page 2: An Illusion of Expansiveness, Jean and Bill Mitchell's Garden (p. 98)
Page 4: A Garden of 1000 Plants, Rosaura Ulvestad's Garden (p. 276)
Page 13: A Perimeter or "Ribbon" Garden, Scott Daigre's Garden (p. 254)

Designed by Judy Geib and Aldo Sampieri

Printed and bound in the United States of America.

2003 2004 2005 2006 2007 / 10 9 8 7 6 5 4 3 2 1

TABLE OF CONTENTS

INTRODUCTION

Great gardens come in all sizes, from vast, formal estates to patches of open land in dense urban settings and even to flower-filled window boxes and hanging baskets. No matter how modest the space, everyone can experience the gift of gardening. California is a land of abundant sunshine and varied climate zones, which in turn inspires a fervent commitment to gardening at every scale. This book celebrates small gardens, reflecting the ingenuity and diversity of taste and style of creative Californians who are using treasured plots of land to express their aspirations and dreams.

Designing gardens in small spaces is different from planting landscapes of half an acre or more. As landscape architect Shirley Kerins explains, details are crucial in a small area. Larger pieces of property often have charming views that can be captured as part of a cultivated garden to become a "borrowed landscape." With a large swath of lawn and foliage extending into the distance, the overall composition becomes more important than the individual elements. In contrast, small gardens are usually located in urban areas. Often walls enclose the property, and the contained yard is the center of attention. Since every element will be scrutinized, it's important to consider each component carefully and to invest in the quality of the materials—slate for the patio, handsome pottery containers, a fine piece of sculpture or a beautiful bench.

In planning a small garden, keep plants small, too, in scale with the space. The design should include trees or large shrubs—the so-called "bones" of a garden—to give a sense of definition or enclosure. Carefully positioned trees and tall shrubs can also mask unattractive aspects of the cityscape. Jeff Britt (see page 66) has used this technique successfully to camouflage phone and utility poles near his San Francisco garden.

Instead of large trees that can overwhelm a small area, select shrubs that can be trained as trees or use dwarf varieties. T'Boo Dalton created a green oasis in the middle of San Francisco by using Australian tree ferns and several other fern varieties (see page 56). Mature trees can become garden features, like the pepper tree in Corrado Giovannoni's Santa Monica garden, where containers of flowering plants are clustered around the trunk (see page 148). Tall plants or those with large leaves or flower clusters should be placed in the rear of the garden with smaller plants in front. Layering—tall plants in back, mid-size in the middle, and smallest reserved for borders—is an exceptionally effective technique for creating the illusion of greater space.

Judy Kameon, owner of Elysian Landscapes in Los Angeles, recommends that the central area of small gardens remain open as lawn or patio, with plants around the perimeter. This strategy gives a sense of generosity and makes the space seem larger. Judy favors planting beds that are at least three feet wide, regardless of length. At this width, plants can be layered comfortably and are easily accessible for maintenance. Many of her designs include built-in benches along one or more borders that provide seating without encroaching on the central space. A particularly striking example is the hilltop garden she designed for Timothy Fryman in Hollywood (see page 260).

Color is an essential component of spatial effects. Bright, bold colors like reds and oranges attract the eye. Cooler colors—pastels, blues, purples—retreat and seem more distant. In a small garden, vivid colors will be more appealing from a distance with cooler colors to lead into the space. However, a few flamboyant focal points can add excitement if used judiciously, as in the colorful entry garden Scott Daigre designed in Los Angeles (see page 254).

Artists often use green to set up a space or to serve as a transition from one color group to another. Gardeners can achieve the same effect with foliage plants. There are many variations of green in leaves—silver, blue, olive, yellow, vivid, pale—as well as variegated patterns in yellow, white, mahogany or even deep burgundy. So many new foliage plants have come on the market that, increasingly, entire gardens are based on foliage. Terry Camiccia likes foliage plants that keep their leaves and animate her Bolinas garden throughout the year. She enjoys pruning and shaping plants into sculptural forms (see page 40). Jean Mitchell has created a sophisticated garden in green and white (see page 98) in her Carmel enclave with foliage plants espaliered against fences and walls. White flowering shrubs and perennials serve as accents.

The new enthusiasm for foliage does not preclude the use of colorful flowers for beautiful small gardens. Many of the gardens in this book were created by passionate plant collectors like Wendy Foster (see page 122) who has filled her walled garden with hundreds of different varieties. Every bit of space is used creatively, and the design is successful because she has combined plants in ways that please the eye and make sense in the space.

Small gardens can be segmented into garden rooms as effectively as larger spaces can. The intent is the same: to entice visitors deeper into the garden where more of its secrets can be revealed. Scott Shrader has accomplished this with dramatic hedges (see page 220); while Ivy Reid made a series of paths through successive vignettes, each with a different theme and purpose (see page 126). Like many California residents, she spends as much time in her garden as possible, moving from one section to another as she pursues a variety of activities.

Dividing a diminutive garden into smaller but unequal spaces will add a sense of scale and dimension. Avoid the temptation to flank the path or entryway with identical plantings. In almost all cases, plants receive varying amounts of light with the result that they will grow into different shapes. Instead, use groups of plants selected for their scale and relationships to one another, and repeat the plant grouping for visual interest. Avoid monotonous plantings like rigid rows of petunias or pansies. Combine in drifts or cluster them for a more natural appearance.

Just as too many plants can overwhelm a small garden, so can a complex design. The smaller the space, the more appropriate it is to define it with simple lines. Geometric lines convey control, which can be tempered with cascading foliage or masses of flowering plants that spill over corners and soften hard edges. Carmel artist Ann Walbert (see page 110) has created her garden in just this way.

In addition to pleasing the eye, gardens should also contribute sweet scents. Fragrant flowers can be placed strategically on trellises, arbors, and pergolas or adjacent to pathways and seating areas. Beware of the "war of the noses," which occurs when too many strongly scented plants are placed in close proximity—jasmine near Angel's Trumpet, for example. One or two fragrant plants will suffice, especially when aromas waft on spring breezes.

Gardens mean different things to different people. Whether you're starting your first one, or redesigning an existing space, take time to think, observe, and plan. First, ask yourself what you want your garden to do. Do you want to grow fresh vegetables? Do you want to fill your house with flowers? Do you want to spend time taking care of plants or do you prefer undemanding plants like succulents, shrubs, or perennials? As a general rule, the more colorful, flowering plants in a landscape, the more time it takes to tend them. If you want a place where you can read or entertain, be sure to reserve some open space.

Once you have defined your objectives, research the types of plants that will thrive in your region. Visit a local public garden to see plants in the landscape rather than in containers in the nursery or garden center. It really helps to see how big plants are when they mature. Observe the sun patterns in your garden so that you will be able to select plants whose requirements for sun and shade match those conditions.

Whatever your plant palette, try to keep it simple. Limiting the number of varieties will ensure that the end result is soothing and relaxing. Before planting, make sure the soil is suitable. Lush, vibrant gardens begin with nutritious soil. The ideal for most plants is called sandy loam, and few places have this condition naturally. Gardeners amend their soil with commercial supplements or planting mixes. Add liberally and work into the soil to a depth of twelve inches or more, and your plants will reward your investment. Every year, add a three to four inch layer of mulch—any organic matter like compost, shredded bark, mushroom compost, cocoa bean hulls or whatever is in abundance in your region—to keep weeds down, retain moisture, and improve soil texture.

These gardening and design guidelines are just that—general guides to creating beautiful, satisfying retreats. But above all, gardens are individual expressions that reflect the interests and personalities of the owners. Our intent is that this book will serve as a visual reference and a source of inspiration, whether you are an experienced gardener or just getting started. We hope the result is that, as you create your own personal Garden of Eden, as you tend your garden, your own life is nurtured and enhanced. May the beauty and goodness that is expressed through the garden also transform the garden of your life.

A CHINESE STYLE GARDEN
HUIE & FRANK YOUNG
DAVIS

orn in China and raised in Taiwan, Huie Young was greatly influenced by her father, Js Liu. A noted architect and artist in Taiwan, he instilled in his daughter an appreciation for beauty and tranquillity. When she and her husband moved to Davis, California, Huie wanted to create a garden that would evoke something of her Chinese heritage. Her garden is small, like those in Taiwan, where land is so scarce and valuable that every corner is landscaped. It is designed as a stroll and viewing garden with distinct destinations linked by transitional elements, all of which can be seen from most rooms in the house.

A fence resembling a Shoji screen encloses the garden, providing privacy and security. A slate patio with a koi pond serves as the transition from house to garden. The bridge over the pond is oriented from north to south, according to the principles of Feng Shui, the Chinese art of placement that determines the siting of rocks, water, plants, and garden ornamentation. The bridge gives another vantage point for viewing water lilies and koi. A curving rock wall is another transitional element, enclosing a "Secret Garden," which symbolizes luck for the beholder. The central element is a richly decorated pagoda enshrining a statue of Buddha.

Huie uses many foliage plants, like Hollywood junipers, precisely trimmed into bonsai and other forms, Japanese pines, and Japanese maple trees. Silver foliage plants

like dusty miller provide shimmering accents. Her plant palette emphasizes pink, yellow, and purple flowers, selected for seasonal color display. Fragrant plants, like sweet olive and wisteria, perfume the garden.

Huie, a professional calligrapher, likes to spend at least three hours each day pruning, deadheading, replanting or grooming potted plants, and just savoring the garden, which awakens precious memories of her childhood and her father.

A ROMANTIC GARDEN WITH JAPANESE INFLUENCES

ALICE CORNING

MILL VALLEY

Alice Corning's garden successfully combines multiple sources, creating what she describes as a "romantic garden with Japanese influences." Over the past twenty-five years, the garden has evolved to include Mediterranean and English elements, and it is now a skillful blend of color, harmony, texture, and rhythm. Although she loves to garden, Alice credits her long-time gardener, Scott Mills, for this successful design.

The property is located in a dense residential area near San Francisco. A wood fence encloses the garden, creating privacy and framing the landscape. The slope is segmented into three distinct levels. At the top is a woodland garden with gingko, flowering cherry, and dogwood trees, underplanted with azaleas, rhododendrons, and shade-loving groundcovers. Here Asian elements—boulders and rock hardscape, carefully placed and sculptured conifers, and a restrained palette—are juxtaposed with an English boxwood hedge.

The second level is a cutting and kitchen garden. In winter, Alice harvests a variety of lettuces, peas, broccoli, and cabbage. In summer, the yield is tomatoes, beans, zucchini, and summer squash. The cutting garden provides ample bouquets of dahlias, hollyhocks, and abundant Oriental poppies that have freely reseeded through much of the garden. On the lower level is a small swath of green lawn, flanked by a formal rose garden containing several dozen hybrid tea roses.

Alice has incorporated a pond filled with goldfish and a bridge, elements of Asian garden design. In place of the traditional water lilies, she prefers bog plants growing in island beds around its perimeter.

A professional potter, Alice takes inspiration for her ceramics from this flower-filled retreat.

A LIVING WORK OF ART

SALLY ROBERTSON

BOLINAS

To Sally Robertson, her garden overlooking the Pacific Ocean is more than a beautiful refuge. It's a living work of art—the inspiration for the botanical watercolors she paints and sells at her Bolinas home and studio. The garden evolved gradually as Sally inserted romantic nooks along the winding paths lined with drifts of undulating and richly fragrant plants.

"I grew up in Northern California and was inspired by San Francisco's Golden Gate Park," she explains. "I wanted to create a small-scale park-like setting with walkways and vignette plantings in my own garden."

Sally uses both hot and cool colors, grouping them by intensity. She favors lavender, blue, rust, and ocher flowers, punctuated by lime green foliage plants like euphorbias. There are dramatic vignettes, like the bed of deep blue scilla beneath a drift of orange daylilies, and surprises at every turn of the path. Among these unexpected elements is an island mound with various types of conifers accented with rocks.

She also appreciates sculptural plants, liberally sprinkling New Zealand flax, agaves, succulents, irises, and daylilies throughout the garden. Roses, too, are favorites, and she selects mildew-resistant varieties like 'Pat Austin' and 'The Edwardian Lady'. She rarely includes annuals, other than California and other poppies that freely reseed every year.

Recently, Sally fulfilled her lifelong dream of creating a pond in her coastal garden. She acquired the neighboring parcel of land and excavated a natural culvert into a 40-foot pond that is now home to darting goldfish, five different types of water lilies, and assorted aquatic plants. Surrounding plantings of ginger, cannas, Japanese iris, and gunnera are reflected on the surface. Willows add grace. Water streams into the pond from a large hewn rock and, at the opposite side, an underwater jet sprays vigorously into the air. A particular mark of success is that the pond has attracted local wildlife, including the endangered red-legged frog.

ON A HIGH MESA

SARAH HAMMOND

BOLINAS

The elegant simplicity of Sarah Hammond's garden belies the challenges of its design. Thirty years ago, when Sarah purchased her property high on a mesa overlooking the Pacific Ocean, much of the land was swampy. Gale force winds, fog rolling in from the ocean, predatory deer, and intermittent drought further limited the prospect of cultivating the site.

Sarah, a garden consultant, skilled gardener, and lecturer, persevered, designing her garden with a simple palette of Mediterranean plants that would tolerate the inhospitable conditions. Evergreen euonymus and pittosporum are precisely pruned into cylinders and ovals, a style of clipping she developed so that the bushes could withstand the wind.

Fifty-five varieties of Old Garden roses grow on trellises and arbors and in the beds, as shrubs or trained as standards. Favorites include the fragrant 'Madame Alfred Carrièr', 'Sombreuil' and hybrid musks 'Penelope', 'Kathleen', and 'Buff Beauty'. The roses are carefully positioned so only one or two are visible from each vista. Beds of catmint 'Walker's Low' bloom in profusion in spring and summer as do several varieties of euphorbia.

Other than the roses, which she waters by hand, Sarah has selected drought-tolerant plants. She applies a deep layer of mulch every year, which also conserves water. This is a non-toxic garden where plants thrive without application of chemical fungicides or pesticides.

Overall, the design is based on structure and form. Its simplicity and repetition of a limited number of plants make the small space seem larger than its 800 square feet. Sarah uses it as a teaching tool and a demonstration garden that illustrates how to create a garden that offers beauty in all seasons. When flowers fade in winter, the structural forms of hedges and shrubs impart a beauty all their own.

ON A CLIFF NEAR THE SEA

TERRY CAMICCIA

BOLINAS

From their house in Bolinas, Terry and Ralph Camiccia have a spectacular view of San Francisco Bay and metropolitan skyline, but the site, high on a cliff near the sea, makes gardening a challenge. For decades, Terry struggled with harsh elements—strong winds and salt air—and battled disease and mildew as she first grew vegetables and later roses. Equally demoralizing was the starkness of the garden in winter when few flowers bloomed. For her third garden, Terry decided to work with rather than against nature, concentrating on trees and shrubs that could be tightly pruned for sculptural beauty and produce green foliage throughout the entire year.

A student of Ikebana, the Japanese art of flower arranging, Terry was impressed by the simple beauty of gardens she visited in Japan. She also admires Italian Renaissance gardens, and she says her garden is a synthesis of the two cultures. Now the garden flows as a series of rooms, linked by a common theme of green leaves. She disavows the notion that foliage can be boring, pointing out the range of light to dark greens and numerous variations like blue-green, gray-green, purple-green, and chartreuse.

Some plants that could flower are so tightly pruned that flowers never form— dusty miller is trained into a round gray ball, and 'Godwin Creek' lavender is similarly shaped before flower spikes appear. Miniature conifers and river privet shrubs are grown in bonsai form as are weeping crabapple and lemon trees. A few flowering plants serve as seasonal accents, like strident magenta cranesbill geraniums that seed themselves throughout the garden. Terry kept a few climbing roses, selecting the most hardy and disease resistant, such as 'Cecile Brunner', which clambers up a tall trellis. A white magnolia climbs up an arbor and scents the spring air with sweet fragrance. Garden ornaments were all crafted by Ralph, who made metal arbors, arches, trellises, and iron seats. Terry spends more time tending to her garden than sitting still. She loves to prune, shape, and tweak the plants and would spend every day at it if she could. "I love my garden—it's my passion," she says.

A HILLSIDE GARDEN

DAVID MCCRORY & ROGER RAICHE

BERKELEY

For David McCrory and Roger Raiche, their hillside garden is both a showcase for their vast plant collection and a laboratory for experimentation. David and Roger are co-owners of Planet Horticulture, a landscape design/build firm based on the property, which was once owned by the distinguished architect Bernard Maybeck. Roger divides his time between the business and his career as a museum scientist with the University of California Berkeley Botanical Garden, where he is in charge of the California native plant collection.

Known for unusual design in both landscapes and container gardens, David and Roger favor a casual and naturalistic approach, preferring foliage to flowering plants. Their personal garden combines California natives and exotic plants from around the world that thrive in the temperate Berkeley climate. They estimate more than 3,000 plants are growing on the quarter-acre site, which is segmented into different garden rooms.

Like many designers, David and Roger create layers of plantings—trees and shrubs in the background, medium size plants in the center, lower growing plants in the foreground, and groundcovers. Native grasses and grass-like plants from South Africa replace manicured lawn, with concrete pavers, interplanted with pennyroyal, and red or variegated leafed clovers as walking surfaces. Species dandelions and New Zealand sedges are used to edge paths.

Himalayan windmill fan palms create a tropical mood. Other trees include conifers, cypress, and Japanese maples. All plants are chosen for their appropriateness

to the site. The rockiest part of the hillside is planted with drought-tolerant rosemary, various varieties of lavender, santolina and Mexican fan palm trees, cacti and succulents. Flowering plants are used sparingly. Lilies, dahlias, and roses like 'Louise Clemens', have been selected so their colors blend in the lush landscape.

Chinese urns, Asian temple artifacts, and Mediterranean olive jars extend the international theme. The garden continues to change and evolve as David and Roger experiment with plant groupings. "We garden by trial and error to see if we like specific plant combinations," David says. "We're constantly refining and improving."

AN OASIS OF LUSH FOLIAGE

T'BOO DALTON

SAN FRANCISCO

From her second floor balcony, T'Boo Dalton looks out on an oasis of lush foliage, hardly typical of metropolitan San Francisco where she lives with her husband, Bernard Stolar. When the couple acquired the narrow site in 1996, there were a few plants struggling to grow on the steep slope behind the house. A wild cherry tree was the principal foundation plant, accompanied by camellias and azaleas, ferns, and a few baby's tears.

Once the property was terraced with fieldstone to create planting beds at three distinct levels, T'Boo turned to the plant selection. She decided to keep the cherry tree and some of the shrubs and added Australian tree ferns and several varieties of terrestrial ferns as the bones of the garden. She likes colorful flowers and plants, but she had to restrict herself to those that would thrive in cool, shady, and often foggy conditions.

Seasonal color comes with the vibrant foliage of Japanese maple trees in fall, followed by camellias and azaleas in winter, and rhododendrons and various flowering bulbs in spring and summer. Chinese lantern is in flower much of the year. Nurtured by a new irrigation system, the baby's tears quickly spread to form thick verdant mounds throughout the garden. This is a restrained garden, soothing in its simplicity, with little ornamentation other than the plants themselves.

This is a low maintenance landscape that requires only pruning and shaping several times a year. T'Boo appreciates its ease of care, which allows her to focus on the equestrian activities that are her principal interest.

A GARDEN FILLED WITH SURPRISES

MANUEL FERNANDEZ

SAN FRANCISCO

From the street, a large Canary Island palm tree looms over Manuel Fernandez's property, giving a hint that this is a garden filled with surprises. Confounding all logic and a cadre of well-meaning advisors, Manuel has created a tropical paradise in San Francisco's cool and foggy climate. Only fifteen years old, the garden already resembles a lush jungle, evoking the time when Manuel lived in the South Pacific. Plants were started mainly from seeds or seedlings so their growth is all the more remarkable.

Manuel attributes his success to selecting plants suitable for the garden's microclimates—a suggestion he offers fellow gardeners wherever they live. By trial and error and shifting plants from one location to another, a determined gardener may find just the right spot for favored plants. Natural underground streams keep the soil moist. By capturing the water, Manuel was able to create favorable conditions for tropical and sub-tropical plants—palms, ferns, banana trees (this area is located in a banana belt, a region with enough humidity for certain banana species to fruit), orchids, and numerous shrubs. Containers of flowering plants, which Manuel changes from season to season, are used as accents.

The site is unusual for San Francisco because the house is situated at the rear of the property. Although the lot is rectangular, the garden consists of different nooks and angles. Manuel offset the path from the street to give the illusion of greater width. Near the front door is a fountain, created by artist Lawrence Kulig, whose cascading water camouflages city noises and attracts birds to drink and bathe.

SEDUCED BY THE SOIL

JEFF BRITT

SAN FRANCISCO

Some people fall in love with houses because of the design; others are attracted by a landscape. Jeff Britt was seduced by the soil. Intrigued by a San Francisco house during a realtor's "open house," he returned with a trowel and dug up some soil in the garden. Once he determined the sandy loam was fertile, he decided to buy the property. Jeff's special interest is professional and personal: an ardent plant collector, he runs a potting soil and fertilizer business.

As soon as he and partner Kevin Ames moved in, Jeff went to work in the garden. As a first step, he removed most of the existing plants so that he could amend the already workable soil. He designed several planting areas on the sloping property where he experiments with a wide range of plants. For color and interest throughout the year, he has created a seasonal progression of flowers and an abundance of colorful foliage. The garden is packed with powerful visuals in part because of his plant mania but also because he believes that an urban garden should focus inward rather than out to the surrounding neighborhood.

Jeff has maximized his space by planting in dense layers. When he sees a "must have" plant at a local nursery, he seizes the moment and the plant and puts it in a pot until he finds a place in the landscape. Like many gardens tended by plant connoisseurs, this is an ever-changing landscape within the constant of the trees and shrubs, the bones

of the garden. Roses are particular favorites, especially 'Buff Beauty' a fragrant Hybrid Musk, 'Graham Thomas', a yellow Austin shrub, and 'Sally Holmes', a vigorous and disease-free white shrub which grows like a climbing rose in warm climates. Viburnum, oak leaf hydrangeas, heuchera, and masses of bluebells thrive in the shade at the bottom of the garden. Flanking a tiny water garden are a Japanese maple tree, geraniums, and irises.

Jeff can survey his handiwork from the patio he built underneath a vintage walnut tree. Here, in the cool summer twilight, he relaxes and reflects on the beauty of his urban garden.

IN A WOODED AREA

BILL PINKERTON

MONTEREY

This gently sloping property has spectacular views of Monterey Bay. The house is in a wooded area, where flower gardens are extremely vulnerable to deer. Bill Pinkerton asked Lynn and Michael Heller to replace the front lawn with a drought- and deer-resistant planting and to design a new approach to the house.

The Hellers created a path up the slope with flat stone pavers for easier walking and steps made of untreated wood landscape ties. Clumps of ornamental feather grass and tufts of blue fescue grasses add motion to the landscape and also provide erosion control for the slope. The grasses replace a traditional lawn, which requires copious amounts of water and fertilizer, and still convey the atmosphere of an inviting green approach to the house.

Trees—maple, olive, and a cedar deodar—define the overall space. Interspersed are hopseed bushes, Australian tea trees, Breath of Heaven, and Princess Flowering shrubs, plants that deer disdain. Groundcovers include cranesbill geraniums that flower most of the year. Among the accents are marguerite daisies, whose small white flowers and gray-green foliage complement burgundy seedpods of the hopseed bushes.

This garden is in harmony with the panoramic view. Maintenance is relatively easy since little water or fertilizer is required. Shrubs are trimmed several times a month to maintain their shapes.

A SHADE GARDEN

DIERDRE SOLARI

CARMEL

Carmel Village is an enclave of small cottages, each with its own unique character and charm. Since land is very expensive, the lots are small and gardening enthusiasts work hard to fulfill their desires for beauty, enjoyment, and the good life. Dierdre Solari commissioned landscape designers Lynn and Michael Heller to transform a backyard dominated by enormous rhododendrons, camellias, and azaleas into a colorful landscape with a profusion of flowers and generous entertaining space.

After removing the overgrown shrubs, the Hellers contoured the land and installed a wall of local Carmel stone to define perimeter planter beds around the lawn. They planted several mature trees and vertical shrubs to anchor the landscape, carefully selecting varieties that would not overwhelm the space. The slow-growing Dragon tree (Dracaena draco) adds a strong silhouette as does a large tree-shaped ivy topiary.

Since this is mainly a shade garden, the planters are filled with shade-loving annuals like primroses and cineraria. Lush ferns serve as backdrops for their vibrant colors. Cannas are tucked in as exclamation points of color. In sunny spots, bright orange, red, and yellow nasturtiums spill over the sides of the planters. Tucked into a corner niche is a small fountain and water garden that adds the cheerful sounds of splashing water to the garden. On the patio, the table and chairs are surrounded by clustered pots of annuals —pansies, violas, and petunias—and succulents like String of Pearls and Wandering Jew.

In this bird-friendly garden, feeders and brightly decorated bird boxes become garden accents. Hummingbirds dart about, sipping nectar from cannas or from feeders suspended from the branches of the ancient oak tree that adds a sense of majesty to the garden.

SANTA BARBARA DAISIES & CARMEL STONE

MICHAELA & JAY HOAG

CARMEL

This lovely entry garden features a mass of Santa Barbara daisies spilling over a three-foot wall of local Carmel stone. When Michaela and Jay Hoag bought property for a summer retreat, the garden had no definition. Landscape designer Richard Hudson developed a plant palette to fulfill Mikey's desire for a beautiful garden that would also provide cut flowers for the house. Mounds of fluffy white daisies now fill the site on both sides of the wall. Complementing them are sweetly fragrant lavender shrubs and cascading Mandeville vines, which produce pink flowers in great profusion throughout the spring and summer months. These plants also serve another purpose—they soften the contours of the rugged stone.

"I like this garden because it's welcoming," Mikey says. "It's also a place where our family gathers and spends time together."

The garden retains its richness and tidy character with an annual shearing back of the shrubs. It's a stunning example of how a small garden can appear larger when multiples of the same plant are used throughout the space.

A TROPICAL SCENE

MARIAN ROSS

CARMEL

A world-traveler, Marian Ross uses her Carmel condominium as a home base. In planning the garden, she asked designers Lynn and Michael Heller to evoke the tropical landscape that captivated her on her travels. The Hellers faced the dual challenge of transforming a long and narrow walkway and undistinguished patio into a lush garden and selecting plants that could create the illusion of a tropical scene in the fog and cool conditions of Monterey.

By selecting plants in scale to the architectural elements and suspending containers from the roof, the Hellers made the path appear more generous. They enlivened the center court with clusters of plants in containers and tucked in a secret fountain and bird feeder. Hundreds of plants have been introduced into the space by using groundcovers, shrubs, annuals, perennials, and trees of varying heights.

Marian requested flowers in purple and deep blue, burgundy, rust, and yellow. Bright pink flowers serve as accents. Begonias, cyclamen, primroses, passion flowers, lobelia, salvia, and camellias provide flowers much of the year. A 'Mr. Lincoln' rose offers richly fragrant deep red blooms from spring through fall. Ferns, succulents, and plants with variegated leaf colors add to the visual drama.

This garden requires weekly maintenance to keep it tidy and welcoming. Each season, the Hellers replace the annual flowers, carefully selecting small plants to maintain the design perspective.

AN ILLUSION OF EXPANSIVENESS

JEAN & BILL MITCHELL

CARMEL

Jean and Bill Mitchell's garden is the epitome of successful small-space design. It's a fascinating use of space both in the ground and on the walls and fences. Jean has capitalized on these vertical surfaces with extensive use of espalier. Along one fence is a Gordon apple whose spring blossoms captivate the eye. In fall, deep red apples are as decorative as they are delicious. Camellias, too, are espaliered, producing walls of glossy green leaves.

Jean created an illusion of expansiveness by limiting the palette to green and white. She is careful to select plants in scale with the space and adds visual interest at eye level with hanging baskets and topiaries. Foliage plants, predominantly in hunter green, provide a serene setting for white flowering plants. Azaleas, which flourish in the Carmel climate, are used as shrubs and standards. There is a formal bed delineated by boxwood containing 'Iceberg' roses as shrubs and trees. Jean loves plants and tucks them into pots and containers everywhere she can. Her favorites include white bacopa trailing from hanging baskets and many different types of ivy.

Each garden vignette includes a small water feature—a fountain and a small pond tucked into the ground and rimmed with tiny green baby's tears. On the patio, there is a rectangular koi pond of raised brick.

An avid gardener for most of her life, Jean has been active in the Garden Club of America and was instrumental in founding the Carmel-by-the-Sea Garden Club after she and Bill moved there in 1974. Jean is quick to point out that her garden requires a high level of maintenance. She enjoys pruning and watering her pots, but she cheerfully admits that as she gets older, she gratefully accepts help from her gardener, whom she has trained to maintain this exquisite garden to her high standards.

A SIMPLE PALETTE OF GREEN, WHITE & LAVENDER

HALLIE & BRAD DOW

CARMEL

Hallie Dow, daughter of Jean Mitchell, and her husband, Brad, live near the Carmel Mission. In planning the garden with Michelle Comeaux, a local landscape architect, the Dows took cues from the architecture and materials of the Mission and the natural slope of their corner lot.

New steps, flanked by terraced planter beds, lead down from the street to the patio and entry garden. Brad Dow and his son-in-law Richard DeAmaral, a third-generation masonry contractor, built these using the adobe brick of the Mission and Michelle Commeaux selected the plants. She also created a dramatic entry through a mature pittosporum hedge that had been planted by previous owners.

A simple palette of green, white, and lavender makes the small space appear larger. Two potato vines flank the front door. Baskets packed with trailing bacopa hang from the eaves over a bed of fragrant lavender edged with Santa Barbara daisies. This design is repeated in the nearby planters, where rosemary cascades over the brickwork. Completing the ensemble are ornamental pots filled with annuals and clustered at various places on the patio.

Two hoary, majestic cypress trees support an inviting hammock strung between their massive trunks. Because this is a low-maintenance garden, there's time to enjoy this garden and gaze out over the nearby lagoon and bird sanctuary.

A BLEND OF COLORFUL FLOWERS

ANN WALBERT

CARMEL

From its beginnings in 1916, Carmel has been known as "the village in a forest." Monterey pines with thick trunks, gray-green Coast live oaks, and evergreen manzanita grew naturally to form dense forest that stretched down to the sandy white dunes. Early settlers added Monterey cypress, coast redwoods, and blue gum eucalyptus. The juxtaposition of gardens—intensely designed and controlled landscapes—in this naturalistic setting is an unusual sight in California. Add to this the creative vision of resident artists, and the result is an array of fascinating gardens.

Among the prettiest is that of painter Ann Walbert, who is well known for her Carmel scenes. Her private garden is a blend of colorful flowers that ebb and flow with the seasons. Hand-painted gates open to an inviting path lined in spring with daffodils blooming in a sea of blue vinca minor. Ann considers color an ally in design, focusing on recessive blues to enlarge her space. She uses agapanthus, iris, delphiniums, catmint and liriope, plants that add visual interest in foliage, texture and shape. California and Iceland poppies, foxgloves, camellias and Douglas irises in raised beds bring late-spring color. They flourish in the semi-shade that covers her garden and most of the village. A large cypress tree dominates the backyard, and Ann puts it to good use. "Gardening underneath a cypress tree is almost impossible, with shade and root factors, so we garden up the tree," she explains. Pots of annuals and succulents are fastened to the bark and watered by a drip irrigation system, a unique solution in a tiny garden.

A WILD POINT OVERLOOKING THE SEA

ROBINSON JEFFERS TOR HOUSE FOUNDATION

CARMEL

Along the coast, on the edge of Carmel, is the stone house and tower built by the noted California poet Robinson Jeffers and his wife, Una. In 1914, when they settled on this wild point overlooking the sea, they planted yew trees evoking their Celtic heritage and created a cutting garden. Although the garden has evolved over the decades, it still functions as a cutting garden, yielding fragrant and colorful flowers for bouquets that fill the rustic house with scent and vibrant color.

The house and garden were designed as a unified whole. Stone windows in the dining room and guest bedroom frame flower-filled vignettes. Outdoors, it's a natural macrocosm in motion—alive with birds, butterflies, and flowers swaying in the wind. Because of the wind and salt sea air, plants were chosen for their hardiness and suitability to the site. California's native wild lilac flourishes along the coastal fog belt, bearing blue flowers in spring. Foundation plants include tree mallows, Love-in-a-mist, scented geraniums, lavender, rosemary, irises and santolina. In spring, a mixture of European and South African bulbs—daffodils, crocosmia, watsonia and lilies—emerge in profusion. There are also numerous drought tolerant plants that thrive in the sandy soil. Plants sprawl and flow through one another in loose patterns, a fitting design for this most unusual naturalistic seaside setting.

Now administered by the Robinson Jeffers Tor House Foundation, the house and garden are open for guided tours on Fridays and Saturdays by appointment.

A WALLED GARDEN WITH A PROFUSION OF PLANTS

WENDY FOSTER

SANTA BARBARA

A thick Eugenia uniflora hedge grows over the rustic brick wall in front of Wendy Foster's house. Visitors who pass through the gate into the tiny walled garden find a profusion of plants flourishing from ground to eye to sky level. Tiny violets wind through Japanese anemones. Begonias of all varieties flourish in the ground and in containers, massed on the patio. Purple and white potato vines climb up stately palm trees.

Jim Melnik, a Santa Barbara landscape designer, assisted Wendy with the plan and plant selection. Every inch of space is carefully utilized, including the brick patio where containers of all sizes are clustered. Although the space is densely planted, the range of greens in the foliage unifies the garden and gives an aura of serenity to the scene. Flowering plants—vining clematis, vivid bougainvillea, Hibiscus 'Itsy Bitsy' and Geranium madarense, a dramatic species of geranium that freely reseeds—add splashes of color throughout the year. A flagstone walk winds through the landscape, past mondo grass, undulating fern fronds, and a majestic Jacaranda tree.

"When I'm indoors, I love looking out at the soothing sea of green," Wendy says. "And I walk through the garden every day to see what's new."

"OUTDOOR ROOMS" & CHARMING VIGNETTES

IVY REID

PACIFIC PALISADES

A series of charming vignettes, connected by meandering paths, surround Ivy Reid's cottage home in Pacific Palisades. She has designed these outdoor rooms as a personal sanctuary, and each is dedicated to one of her myriad interests and activities. Each vignette contains a seating area and a water feature, both to attract birds and to add the soothing sounds of water to the harmonious setting.

In one, she dines. She loves to cook, so in another she grows fresh herbs and vegetables. There is a cozy nook where she serves afternoon tea to fortunate guests. Another area is filled with flowers she harvests to dry, press, and use for greeting cards and other gifts from her garden. The entire space is filled with flowering annuals, perennials, shrubs, and vines. A special section is dedicated to perennials, another to cutting flowers. And a shady nook filled with hydrangeas, hostas, hellebores, foxgloves, and ferns reminds her of her childhood home in New England. Fragrance is important, too, and rich scents of datura, gardenias, jasmine, and roses permeate the air. A special Moon Garden, filled with white flowers, is a favorite spot for evening repose.

All this sounds like an estate garden, but Ivy skillfully created these vignettes around her modest two-bedroom house on an urban lot. Pathways lead through vignette after vignette, each densely planted in layers. Taller shrubs and perennials are in the background, mid-size plants in the middle, and small perennials and annuals in the foreground.

It might seem that a garden this lush and full would need a lot of maintenance, but Ivy says it isn't so. She gardens organically so the soil is rich in nutrients. She has selected plants that are naturally resistant to diseases and those that attract beneficial insects to prey on harmful bugs. Her main chores are in spring and fall, when she cuts back shrubs and perennials, replaces annuals, and spreads out organic fertilizer. The plants grow so densely that there is no room for weeds. All this gives Ivy time to enjoy her creation. "My garden is my place of refuge, where I heal and nourish my body, mind, and soul, where I can create beauty for myself and to share with others," she says.

A DESERT GARDEN

GARY LYONS

BURBANK

Gary Lyons is one of the world's leading authorities on cacti and succulents. He is the curator of the Desert Garden at the Huntington Botanical Gardens in San Marino, a Fellow of the prestigious Linnean Society of London, and a dedicated member of the International Union for Conservation of Natural Resources. His urban garden is as much a laboratory, observation, and conservation space as it is an ornamental display of his collection of some two thousand cacti and succulent species.

Enclosed by a wood fence for privacy and security, the backyard is planned for optimal display. Pathways of brick shards provide access through the plants for viewing and ease of handling, although some specimens are so spiny that they require great care. Some of the plants—like the immense cereus—are at least fifty years old. Two beaucarania, started from seed in 1972, are now fifteen feet tall.

Many plants grow in clay pots so that Gary can control their sun and water requirements, which is especially helpful when winters are colder and wetter than these plants prefer. He can move them around if varying sun or shade conditions impact their health. Pots also allow Gary to change their groupings as he experiments with different visual effects. Sometimes he stacks pots on one another to better display certain specimens. He also brings plants to his lectures and workshops to use as teaching tools.

Gary spends a great deal of time in this garden, studying and observing the plants. He also does some breeding, creating unique hybrids. At least twenty percent of the plants in his collection are endangered or threatened in the wild.

A COTTAGE GARDEN

MAUREEN McMORROW

SOUTH PASADENA

When Maureen McMorrow and her husband, Ken Weinberg, bought their craftsman-style house in South Pasadena, the backyard was dominated by an enormous avocado tree in the middle of a scraggly lawn. For the next ten years, Maureen tried valiantly to garden but nothing thrived beneath the 35-foot tall tree. Finally she consulted landscape architect Shirley Kerins, who designed a cottage garden in keeping with the architecture of the house.

Kerins transformed the small, flat area into a richly textured urban retreat that includes a patio and spa, a water garden, and numerous planting beds. The garden looks full because planters vary in height. Plants cluster around the bottom of the four-foot stone planters, and the eye is drawn upward to view plants growing at a higher level. Trellises and arbors and bamboo teepees provide structure for climbing roses and sweetly scented jasmine vines.

One planter bed is reserved for Ken, who concentrates on vegetables. Spring bounty includes Swiss chard, lettuce and squash. Modern and heirloom tomatoes appear in summer, followed by gourmet lettuce varieties and heirloom beets in fall.

Maureen grows seventy-two varieties of roses. Some are climbing roses covering the fence. Others are in planter beds, while miniature roses are tucked into pots and clustered in containers. Her favorites include 'Ballerina' and 'Lyda Rose'.

A decomposed granite pathway flanked with Baby's Tears leads visitors through the garden to the spa and seating area. A river-rock wall capped with Bouquet Canyon stone separates the spa from the garden, but the surrounding roses add fragrant color to the corner nook.

EVIDENCE OF AN ITALIAN HERITAGE

CORRADO GIOVANNONI

SANTA MONICA

Corrado Giovannoni's Italian heritage is very much in evidence in the gardens he designs in the Los Angeles area. His own garden in Santa Monica incorporates many of the principles he uses professionally to create the illusion of spaciousness and generosity in a small area. His design and plant selection give this garden a timeless quality that makes it seem as though it has always been there. In reality Corrado began only five years ago, faced with an unkempt lawn and a majestic California pepper tree.

In reconfiguring the space, Corrado took advantage of the natural slope and introduced new levels by building a stone retaining wall and adding a series of steps at the property line. At the top of the steps he installed an ornamental fountain on the wall of the neighboring garage. He has divided the garden into two distinct areas, one closer to the house for entertaining and the other more distant and secluded. The seating area is defined by shrubs and surrounded by colorful and lush flowering plants with the original pepper tree as a focal point. His favorite shrubs include privet, sweet olive, and viburnum. The ground surface is decomposed granite rather than grass to reduce watering and maintenance, particularly sweeping up the leaves from the pepper tree. Corrado has clustered containers of flowering plants around the base of the tree, a strategy that allows him to make use of the area occupied by the roots. This also protects the tree from overwatering since he can water the pots directly. Among his favorites are hydrangeas, gardenias, and particularly geraniums. These have become his signature plants, in part because he grew up surrounded by them in Italy.

A stone path leads to the more secluded area. Its entrance is defined by an arbor covered with 'Cl. Joseph's Coat', a riotously colored rose with vivid orange and red blooms. Shrubs conceal a deck with a hot tub and lounging space.

Corrado encourages his clients to include garden ornaments in the landscape design. In his own garden, he has added a touch of whimsy by suspending a birdcage planted with ivy from the pepper tree. He likes to use what he has on hand, but in an unexpected way. A discarded picture frame now encloses an orchid plant to create a living picture. Overall, his is a garden filled with beauty and accented with fun.

A MEDITERRANEAN STYLE GARDEN

CATRIONA DAVIS & DEAN KUBANI

SANTA MONICA

Catriona Davis and her husband, Dean Kubani, commissioned Corrado Giovannoni to design their garden in a classic Mediterranean style to complement the Spanish architecture of their house. Corrado created an entry courtyard with a central fountain and seating along the wall. He replaced the lawn with decomposed granite walkways, using the dirt from the excavation to contour the ground. A 3 1/2-foot stucco wall encloses the garden, providing privacy and insulation from street noise.

This is a classic courtyard garden filled with flowers and alive with butterflies and hummingbirds. Two mature melaleuca trees provide shade for benches near the fountain. Foliage plants, such as non-fruiting olive trees and hopseed bushes, with leaves in shades of green, gray green and deep green predominate. The flowers are white and lavender with a little pink and bright yellow added as vivid accents. Lavender, rosemary, salvia, butterfly bush, and 'Iceberg' roses provide color and fragrance most of the year.

The garden needs just a few hours of tending each month—mainly removing old blooms from roses and lavender. The shrubs and perennials require very little water and fertilizer.

Every fall, Corrado shears back the perennials and shrubs and adds mulch to the beds. This garden provides maximum enjoyment with a modest investment of effort.

A LUSH TROPICAL GARDEN

ROBYNN ABRAMS

SANTA MONICA

Robynn Abrams knew nothing about plants when she moved to Santa Monica from her native New York. That all changed when she discovered the riotously colored plants that flourish in Southern California. With advice from a local landscape designer, Robtnn created a lush tropical scene that surrounds her modest house. "When friends from the East Coast visit, they tell me they feel like they're on a vacation," she says.

Like many Southern California residents, Robynn wanted to extend the interior of the house with a series of garden rooms. Plants with dark green foliage and cranberry colored flowers thrive in her front garden. She layered the space with tall cannas and shrubs in the background and lower growing perennials in the foreground. Ornamental grasses like pennisetum add movement and foliage interest.

A Mexican blue gate leads to a side garden, which Robynn designed to resemble the rocky bed of a dry stream. Her father was a keen fisherman, and, in his memory, Robynn included his favorite fishing rod. This space also serves as a transition to the back garden, which is connected to the house by French doors. It's filled with euphorbias and other low-care plants, many originating from a similar Mediterranean climate. She also likes hot tropical colors and uses bright splashes of colorful cannas with great abandon. An ornamental banana tree anchors one corner of the back garden, which is defined by a brick wall supporting a passion fruit vine. Tall ginger plants add another tropical note.

As a new, self-taught gardener, Robynn was particularly pleased when her garden was included in a recent benefit garden tour.

AN OASIS WITH PALMS & TWIN POOLS
NANCY GOSLEE POWER
SANTA MONICA

Nancy Goslee Power is one of the most respected landscape designers in California. Her award-winning firm has created hundreds of gardens, from small to grand, private and public, including the master plan for the Los Angeles Arboretum. As a designer, her goal is to create gardens that fit their sites and reflect the needs of their users.

An interior designer in New York before moving to Santa Monica in 1977, Nancy has a strong sense of color and form, which complements her deep knowledge of plant materials. Her designs reflect her world travels and her experiences with diverse cultures, landscapes, and ecologies. In small spaces, she emphasizes that it is essential to consider every detail.

In her own garden, she has concentrated on creating a space for entertaining. Her gatherings can include just a few close friends or more than a dozen. She believes in unifying house and garden, often with French doors. In her Santa Monica house, each room has at least one French door, open to breezes . Guests drift freely from the kitchen to a seating area with a built-in bench covered with colorful pillows. A roof covers part of the patio, and an outdoor fireplace creates an inviting and comfortable place where Nancy and her guests can enjoy the garden even on chilly evenings by the sea.

The enclosed garden is also a spa, a palm-filled oasis with twin pools. One is a spa tub. The other is a water garden, complete with goldfish, water lilies, and irises. Raised planter beds contain drought-tolerant plants. Nearby, pendulous and fragrant angels' trumpet flowers fill the area with a hauntingly sweet scent, complemented by the rich bouquet of lilies.

AN ORNAMENTAL EDIBLE GARDEN
BARBARA McCARREN & JUD FINE
VENICE

I n planning their entry garden, sculptors Barbara McCarren and Jud Fine surveyed their property from an unusual perspective: they climbed out on the roof of their Venice house to see the landscape from above. Undeterred by the conventional wisdom that vegetable gardens should be hidden from view, they designed an ornamental edible garden that encourages visitors to stroll through and savor luscious vegetables and herbs.

"We needed the space behind the house for our studio," Barbara explains. "The front is the sunniest location so that's where we decided to grow our vegetables."

A thick ficus hedge masking a chain link fence provides privacy and security for the densely planted space. The garden is planned around five raised beds, artfully constructed and filled to overflowing with vegetables, herbs, and flowers. These are connected by paths of irregular sandstone pavers set in the earth. Lime and orange trees anchor the garden at the perimeter.

Barbara grows many of her favorite vegetables from seed, some saved from the previous harvest. Early Girl, Better Boy, and Sweet 100 tomatoes produce masses of green vines and ruby red tomatoes. Dusky purple eggplants, Golden Bush zucchinis, and frilly leaves of glossy lettuce plants provide color and fresh produce throughout the summer months. During the mild winter, Barbara and Jud plant and harvest carrots, broccoli, peas, and mesclun lettuces.

Zinnias and marigolds add vivid color—oranges, yellows and pinks—and protect the vegetables from insects. In fall and winter, the palette is more subdued, with flowers in purple and lavender hues.

A DROUGHT TOLERANT GARDEN

DAN GRAEF

VENICE

When Dan Graef bought his Venice property in 1969, the house had a traditional front lawn and a few shrubs near the door. Today, the space has been transformed into a striking Mediterranean setting focused on a dramatic bed of rocks and succulents and incorporating at least two hundred species of drought-tolerant plants. The project began modestly when Dan discovered he had run out of room in his back garden and placed one of his favorite succulents in the front lawn. It looked so good that he added another, and another, until he decided to remove the lawn entirely.

A professional cabinetmaker, Dan is especially interested in structure and textures. He focuses on what he describes as "voids and volumes of plants," instead of massing them in beds. He is as fascinated with how plants occupy space as he is with leaf textures and colors. Flowers are secondary to his design approach. When they emerge in spring, he regards them as a bonus rather than the reason for his garden. He is careful to group plants with contrasts in foliage texture or leaf or flower color. One of his most successful combinations is the dark purple spikes of Pride of Madeira against the bright pink flowers of Madagascar geraniums. These are two of his favorites, and he propagates hundreds from cuttings and seeds of the parent plants.

In designing the garden, Dan built a fence of natural wood adjacent to the sidewalk and walkways of earth and ground bark within his space. Along the fence, he installed planter boxes for annuals, which he changes out three times a year. He also planted nineteen eucalyptus trees to provide shade near the house.

The garden attracts a great deal of attention from neighbors and visitors and is frequently included in garden tours. "The social aspect of my garden was completely unexpected," Dan says. "Whenever I'm working in the garden, people stop to talk about the plants, some of which they've never seen before." He delights in sharing gardening information and offers cuttings and seedlings to interested visitors, in the time-honored custom of spreading the garden beyond its confines.

A SERIES OF INTIMATE PLACES

STANLEY NOWAK & SUSIE KANG

VENICE

Landscape and floral designer Susie Kang collaborated with her husband, Stanley Nowak, to renovate their Venice garden into a series of intimate spaces connected by a meandering path that encourages visitors to stroll through the lush plantings that unfold from space to space.

Raised planting beds are central to their design. "Most suburban gardens are too flat, " Stanley says. "It's important to raise the planting surfaces by elevating the beds." In addition to enhancing visual interest, this strategy also broadens the walking area, allowing freer movement along the paths.

Stanley and Susie selected mature trees to anchor the space, including date palms and silk floss trees, which they admire for their textured trunks. Rocks and boulders, carefully matched for contour, size, and color, define the planter areas and add texture. Crevices and niches are filled with groundcovers that spill over onto the path.

Mediterranean plants predominate in the garden. In addition, Susie and Stanley admire the sculptural forms of succulents, which they use to great effect—clambering up tree trunks, sprawling as groundcovers, clustered in pots around seating areas. They are serious, adventurous gardeners who create unusual combinations like hydrangeas and small succulents or wax begonias.

Their interest in natural objects like rocks and boulders extends to their garden furniture. One of their favorites is a two-tiered table constructed with slabs of Malibu sandstone resting on Malibu shale stone. These complement the walls of the planters to give a sense of solidity and permanence to the space.

THINKING SMALL

JAN BRILLIOT

VENICE

Designers Jay Griffith and Russell Cletta thought small in virtually every aspect of planning Jan Brilliot's garden. "Small space, small plants, and a small budget," Jay recalls. "Jan wanted a working garden true to the style of the 1920s Spanish bungalow house and one that would wear well and be as cost-effective as possible."

To keep costs low, Griffith and Cletta reused as much material as possible on the property and selected very young plants and trees. "Many people don't realize that plants can grow incredibly fast," Jay says. "It's not necessary to start with mature ones."

A perimeter hedge of myoporum, which grew from seedlings to a dense 10-foot hedge in just 36 months, creates a sense of privacy and enclosure that makes the small space seem bigger. Within, the compact garden is enhanced by layered planting—a citrus allee borders the hedge and in turn is bordered by a vegetable garden. Variegated and red-leafed cannas, accented by agaves, complete this vignette.

The design achieves a sense of depth through foreground planting of a single row of purple-leafed plum trees that are kept open and lacy in shape. To create the patio, Griffith and Cletta broke up the concrete of an unused driveway and interplanted it with evergreen sedum. The citrus allée is visible from the patio and another orchard at the rear of the property enhances the perspective.

A water garden installed by a previous owner has been transformed into a dry pond containing agave with blue foliage to suggest the sense of water. Drought-tolerant succulents and foliage plants predominate, providing rich color—red, orange, blue, and green—with minimum maintenance.

SERENITY & ANTIQUES

SUE BALMFORTH

VENICE

Interior designer Sue Balmforth lives in a small (1,500-square-foot) house in Venice, but she has extended the living space by building several patios and a 30-foot lap pool, surrounded by lush gardens. Flowers are everywhere in this compact landscape. There are two hundred rose bushes, planted in the ground, twining over custom arbors, and filling antique urns. Hydrangeas, delphiniums, fragrant jasmine and honeysuckle vines, and pretty pansies and other annual flowers accent them.

Sue's garden is both a serene retreat for relaxing and entertaining and a setting for her antiques business, which is called Bountiful after the town in Utah where she was born and raised. She specializes in French, English and American nineteenth-century painted furniture, with an emphasis on garden furniture and artifacts. Her private garden is her showplace, where she can display garden ornaments and furnishings to their best advantage. Of particular interest is a selection of wicker furniture colorfully decorated with floral cushions and pillows made from vintage 1920s fabric.

"I have flowers everywhere, in the garden, and on all the furniture," she says.

Her house and garden are filled with long-stemmed, vibrant roses like 'Fame', 'Brandy', and 'First Prize'. Her favorite is the acclaimed 'Yves Piaget', from the renowned House of Meilland. She has sixty-five bushes, enough to decorate outside and indoors. Sue capitalizes on vertical space by including arbors, covered with climbing versions of

'Iceberg', 'Joseph's Coat', and 'First Prize'. Twenty-six fragrant 'Lillian Austin' roses have been grafted as 4-foot tree roses, making their fragrant flowers easy to enjoy. A mass planting of forty 'Johann Strauss' bushes, an old-fashioned looking floribunda with candy pink flowers, lends a delightful lemon verbena fragrance to the garden.

Sue expands the space with mirrors of her own design. A craftswoman, she makes custom mirrors using nineteenth-century ceiling tin reclaimed from older buildings and wood from barn floorboards.

FOR A SITE ALONG A CANAL

GARY HILL

VENICE

Like its Italian namesake, Venice is a network of scenic canals by the sea. Flower gardeners have to overcome significant atmospheric obstacles to fill their yards and homes with blooms. Gary is a sketch artist, designer, and enthusiastic gardener who has filled his front garden with hundreds of different plants, carefully selected for their suitability to the site along the canal.

The landscape resembles a butterfly with outspread wings with a center lawn enclosed by undulating borders of flowering plants. Two Tamarisk trees and a fig tree remain from the original garden. Gary added honeysuckle and roses, hydrangeas and viburnum, datura and false heather, and a spectacular Pride of Madeira, whose fat spikes of deep blue flowers are magnets for bees and butterflies.

Some roses can withstand the fog and salt air without any traces of disease and flower freely. Gary prefers 'Iceberg', 'Sally Holmes', which grows as a sprawling climbing rose, 'Graham Thomas' for its vivid yellow and fragrant flowers, and 'Garden Party', as well as a few old reliables—'Tiffany' and 'China Doll'. Another favorite plant is star clusters, which produces clusters of tiny star-shaped flowers much of the year.

Gary's small garden is densely planted, but the effect is not overwhelming. The lawn gives a sense of expansiveness and serves as a transition between the various plant groupings. The restrained palette, mainly green and white, sparingly accented with color creates a serene and inviting space.

A STYLIZED DESERT GARDEN

PHILLIP DIXON & VERONIQUE VIART

LOS ANGELES

A professional photographer whose assignments take him around the world, Phillip Dixon is fascinated by the domestic architecture of the indigenous peoples of the Middle East and Central America. He based his own house in Los Angles on these simple dwellings, which integrate indoor and outdoor space. A massive white wall encloses the property, completely masking house and garden within. The house itself is built around a central courtyard and pool. Rooms flow from one another in an open plan, free of doors. Because the house is below grade, steps lead down from the courtyard to the ornamental, but functional, pool and adjacent living spaces.

In the garden, Phillip wanted plants appropriate for the Mediterranean climate of Los Angeles and the architecture of the house. Because of his travel schedule, he planned a stylized desert garden that requires little maintenance. He favors the clean sculptural lines of cacti that he collects. Dragon trees, pipe organ cactus, century plant, cereus, and agaves dominate the landscape. His foundation planting of a specimen dragon tree is so hardy that the plant freely reseeds and has spread throughout the garden.

The rugged, simple forms of the rocks and boulders Phillip has included in the beds complement the angular shapes of the plants. Massive urns are placed at strategic viewing sites.

This unusual house and garden type, popular in Mexico, South America, and the Middle East, is seldom seen in America, but it can be adapted to regions with mild winters.

"OUTDOOR ROOMS"

SCOTT SHRADER

LOS ANGELES

L andscape designer Scott Shrader has created a lush green sanctuary in a dense urban part of Los Angeles. When he purchased his house four years ago, Scott replaced the existing garden with three outdoor rooms, each opening from a room of the small house. "This technique makes both house and garden seem larger," he explains. To achieve his design, Scott planted ficus shrubs around the perimeter of the lot and trained them into a dense twelve-foot hedge that matches the height of the house. French doors opening from the living room, dining room, and den extend the interior space seamlessly into the garden.

The garden itself is partitioned with two eight-foot hedges, each with a broad opening in the center to allow easy circulation within the garden. Pairs of seventeenth-century French limestone fence posts mark these entrances. Although this is a new garden, it achieves a timeless quality through the use of carefully chosen antiques and decorative objects, creating juxtapositions of stone, ceramic, wood, and metal. Specimen plantings include non-fruiting olive trees, agaves, and orchids.

The central garden room features a water lily pool with a soapstone fountain that serves as a base for a bronze statue of Icarus. Vivid orange Japanese goldfish in the pool add color and movement to the design.

Nineteenth-century Guatamalan paving tiles cover the ground in the center garden while gravel is used in the side gardens. All dirt surfaces are camouflaged for a clean, simple appearance. Overall, the effect of this sophisticated garden is that of a meticulously designed setting, both for entertaining and for private contemplation

A PROFUSION OF COLOR

SUNNY & SUSAN ESTRADA

LOS ANGELES

When Sunny and Susan Estrada bought their Los Angeles property ten years ago, the backyard was completely untouched. As professional designers, the Estradas knew that the first step was to define how they would use the garden. To make the garden private and welcoming they planted a screen of ficus hedges and modified the adjacent driveway by planting grass in channels cut in the concrete. The garden itself includes a broad swath of lawn on which children can play, with planting beds around the perimeter and a deck for dining and entertaining. The deck also serves another purpose in masking a low spot at the rear of the house.

The undulating edges of the planting areas incorporate concrete rubble salvaged from the devastating earthquake of 1994. The water garden is designed as a waterfall and a freeform pond executed in concrete accented with stone. Water lilies, aquatic plants, and goldfish enliven the waterfall and pool.

A small garden looks larger when plants are layered, and the Estradas skillfully use this technique. Perimeter plantings consist of tall shrubs and small trees in the background—variegated pittosporum, purple-flowered Princess Flowering tree, liquid amber tree, and a lemon tree—while smaller plants in the foreground command attention. A rose-lover, Sunny has included fifty bushes in the back garden. Roses bloom in profusion in beds, along arbors, and over trellises. Susan loves vibrant oranges and yellows, and

colorful flowers abound. Nasturtiums twine gracefully around borders and seating areas. Mexican marigolds, various salvias, 'Gypsy Dancer', 'Mandy', 'Lucille Ball', and Chris Evert' roses are among their favorites. When the garden itself is filled, they cluster pots and containers around the potting bench and deck.

"Our gardens are known for a profusion of pure color," says Susan. "We like color and we aren't afraid to use it."

FORM & FRAGRANCE

MELISSA MILLER & RENE ENGEL

LOS ANGELES

Melissa Miller and Rene Engel envisioned a garden that would complement the architecture and interiors of their Spanish revival style house, which is furnished in Monterey style accented with vintage cowboy artifacts. Melissa collects vivid Bauer pottery from the 1920s, which she intended to display indoors and out.

Melissa and Rene collaborated with Kathy Glascock, a noted Los Angeles landscape designer, to create a versatile outdoor living space and a handsome setting for the collection. As a basis, they incorporated the brick patio and the majestic avocado tree that had been part of the original garden. A ramada shades the seating area and supports a vibrant Cup of Gold vine. Pots are clustered around walkways and artfully arranged on the wall of Rene's studio.

The garden is carefully designed to give the illusion of greater space by means of layered plants, with taller shrubs in the background and smaller ones in front. Melissa prefers form to flowers—structural and textural plants—and includes numerous types of succulents and cacti in her garden. Fragrance is important as well. In the evening, the rich perfume of pendulous Angel's Trumpet flowers scents the air. Lanterns suspended from the overhanging avocado tree enhance the romantic ambiance.

With a dual career in interior design and psychotherapy, Melissa has a full schedule, but she makes sure to garden every week. "It's my therapy," she says, "and I tell my patients to make gardening part of their therapy, too."

A WILD TROPICAL GARDEN

LAURA COOPER & NICK TAGGART

LOS ANGELES

As artists, both Laura Cooper and her husband, Nick Taggart, draw inspiration from their garden. They collaborated on the design, transforming a barren slope into a wild and tropical garden by creating a series of terraced planting beds and steps. "People worry about plants sliding on slopes, but it's not too complicated to build retaining walls and improve the soil," Nick says. "Hillside gardens can be very interesting because paths can wind up and around and the vista becomes an extension of your own landscape."

Soil excavated to make the steps is now used in the raised beds they constructed on the steepest slopes. Laura and Nick amended this native soil with compost, a byproduct from the chickens they raise for fresh eggs.

Red and orange flowers enliven the hillside. Nasturtiums creep along pathways; canna 'Tropicana' provide vertical exclamation points of color; roses like 'Taboo' and 'Ingrid Bergman' add bold reds as accents. Under a floss silk tree is an area of sun-dappled shade for ferns and other shade-loving plants.

Laura has fallen in love with plants and frequently brings home new treasures. She tucks them here and there, creating what she describes as a Persian carpet of plants, accented with purple or blue flowers. She is careful to emphasize the architectural character of the design with sculptural plants like aloes, agaves, aeoniums, and other succulents. She juxtaposes them with what she calls soft, atmospheric plants—ornamental grasses and delicate fennel that sway in the breezes. "You need form against the frothiness," she explains.

A YEAR-ROUND RETREAT

PAUL & SUSAN ROBBINS

LOS ANGELES

An English horticulturalist, Paul Robbins now lives and works in Los Angeles. He moved to California in 1996, enchanted both by the warm climate and by Susan Woods, who soon became his wife. In their backyard, which had been almost entirely concrete, Paul designed a garden that has become their year-round retreat from the surrounding urban environment.

Podocarpus hedges now camouflage the block walls. In addition to creating privacy, the hedge also softens the space and absorbs some of the street noise. Carefully placed trees frame views of nearby majestic palms and screen out rooflines of neighboring houses and telephone lines.

Within the garden, Paul extended the bedroom living space by adding a wooden deck and pergola. A limestone terrace two steps below the deck serves as a dining area. Flagstone paths, interplanted with creeping thyme, connect the terrace to several outdoor rooms and secret seating spaces. "Even a small garden can create a bit of expectation and surprise if you hide spaces," Paul says.

The plant palette is simple, focusing on plants that thrive in Southern California's Mediterranean climate—verbena, salvia, lavender, mullein, and ornamental grasses, including feather grass and silver grass. Orange trees bear fruit most of the year. Throughout the garden, large terra cotta urns and jars serve as focal points. Some are empty while others contain bamboo and other foliage plants. By limiting the plant palette and introducing simple but massive forms as ornaments, Paul has instilled a sense of cohesiveness throughout the garden that expands the small space.

A LUSH, FLOWER-FILLED SANCTUARY

ALEX STEVENS & PAMELA BERSTLER

LOS ANGELES

The talented husband and wife team of Alex Stevens and Pamela Berstler designs landscapes throughout greater Los Angeles. In their own garden, Pamela says, "We designed by and for our pleasure."

Since Alex and Pamela live and work in the building they own in West Los Angeles, they needed a refuge from the pressures of their business and from the bustling city streets. Together they have created a lush, flower-filled sanctuary with secret spots and special nooks.

By building trellises in strategic spots, Alex and Pamela established a sense of enclosure. Vines of various kinds—passion flower, trumpet, and bower vines—gracefully define the openings and beckon visitors to individual destinations. A meandering path leads through hundreds of flowering plants and dramatic foliage plants. Just a short walk down the path makes Pamela feel as though she's gone on a vacation to a plant lover's paradise.

Over time, the plant palette has evolved from herbs and edibles to ornamentals—many Old Garden and modern roses including fragrant 'Double Delight', 'Love Potion Number Nine' and 'Gemini', Shasta daisies, irises, Mexican marigolds, agaves, and numerous succulents.

In one vignette, a mirror reflects vines and roses across the seating area and gives the illusion of a larger space. In another, Alex and Pamela built what they call "succulent boxes," where plants grow in a container resembling a picture frame to become a living painting.

Every morning Alex and Pamela have breakfast in their garden, watching as it unfolds from day to day, season to season in dramatic splashes of color and movement.

A PERIMETER OR "RIBBON" GARDEN

SCOTT DAIGRE

LOS ANGELES

"Short and squat" was Scott Daigre's first impression of the front yard of the Los Angeles house he shares with Sam Hamann. A landscape designer and an ardent plant collector, Scott was determined to transform the space into an attractive display area for his plants.

In replacing front lawn with landscape beds, Scott took advantage of the gentle slope from the house to the sidewalk. Rather than planting close to the house, he sited the garden at the perimeter of the property and built a freeform "ribbon of garden" that wraps from the front and along the entire side. The border creates a sense of privacy and definition, much as a hedge or fence would, but this approach gives vibrancy and movement to the space.

Scott uses roses as the foundation plants—favorites include 'Brown Velvet', 'Brass Band', 'Artistry', 'Olympiad', 'Taboo', 'Brandy' and 'Ambridge Rose'—and adds flowering plants, with an emphasis on reds and oranges, as seasonal accents. In spring, ranunculus and daffodils are a riot of color. Following are tall spikes of iris and bright orange crocosmia. Daylilies, Jupiter's beard, plectranthus argentatus, succulent perennials like echeveria and agaves add foliage and sculptural drama.

Scott has created vignettes along the driveway and in the backyard, where edible plants like artichokes are included for both harvest and beauty. He is partial to eccentric garden ornaments, making a birdfeeder from a shovel and using a cast-iron sugar kettle as a water feature. Well-worn watering cans and dilapidated ladders become garden accents. In his professional life, he encourages clients to express their own creativity and personality by including objects that have meaning for them. "Gardens aren't static," Scott says. "There are no rules in my garden. It creates itself as it goes along."

A GARDEN WITH CLEAN, SIMPLE LINES

TIMOTHY FRYMAN

LOS ANGELES

Timothy Fryman's property in the Hollywood Hills offers stunning views over the city. To capitalize on the site, Timothy commissioned a garden from Judy Kameon, owner of Elysian Landscapes, who is known for creative contemporary designs. Judy converted the flat plateau into a captivating space using a California Modern vocabulary with clean, simple lines for the hardscape features and a palette of plants with sculptural interest and minimal maintenance requirements.

Large rectangular pavers interplanted with broad bands of lawn were installed in the flat space with plants around the perimeter. Larger shrubs planted on the upper edges of the hillside capture additional space and create the illusion of a larger garden. Ornamental grasses like dwarf pampas, flax, purple fountain grass, and golden junipers are carefully placed to frame vistas. Other plants include kangaroo paws, agaves, aoniums, Bird of Paradise, daylilies, and silver leafed artemesia and dusty miller.

A masonry retaining wall extends from the house to the edge of the property forming a continuous planting bed filled with easy care foliage plants. A built-in mahogany bench is placed in front of the bed, adjacent to the patio. When Timothy entertains, he adds a table in front of the bench where he and his guests can dine, surrounded by the wonderful views in this remarkable garden.

TIMOTHY FRYMAN   265

A SOPHISTICATED COTTAGE GARDEN

SANDRA TAYLOR

LOS ANGELES

For her entry, Sandra Taylor envisioned a garden with country charm, and yet it had to be appropriate for sophisticated, urban Los Angeles. She requested the flowers found in an old-fashioned English cottage garden—roses, hollyhocks, irises, daylilies, and the like—but in a more urbane design.

In response, landscape designer Judy Horton developed a formal plan based on six parterres surrounded by gravel paths with a brick walk leading from the street to the front door. She filled the beds with old-fashioned looking modern roses, with fragrance and billowing blossoms, and companion plants selected for complementary color and style. Maintenance is simple since every plant is easily accessible in the compact (6 x 6 feet or 8 x 8 feet) parterres.

A wisteria planted in a massive container becomes a focal point at the end of the path. At the perimeter, a white picket fence separates the private garden from the public space. A row of irises lines the sidewalk with a bed in front filled with cottage plants like hollyhocks, cosmos, verbascum, and seasonal annuals. 'Cl. New Dawn' grows above the front door, and a large shrub, 'Sparrieshoop', cascades gracefully in a corner. David Austin English roses are combined with perennials like purple salvias and magenta cranesbill geraniums. The result is a recreation of an English cottage garden skillfully interpreted for an urban site.

DESERT AMBIANCE & MOOD

JAKE SCOTT & RHEA RUPERT

LOS ANGELES

Jake Scott and Rhea Rupert particularly enjoy the high desert regions of California. When they decided to redesign their Los Angeles property, they commissioned Judy Kameon of Elysian Landscapes to capture the desert ambiance and mood. Judy's ingenious solution is based on a translucent acrylic panel screen, tall enough to provide security and privacy, and back-lit to glow at night. By enclosing the space with the screen and resurfacing the driveway with stained concrete to resemble a patio, she created an outdoor room that welcomes guests to the house even before they reach the front door.

The screen also provides space for a double-sided planting border. The street side features purple foliaged nandina, accented with deep blue lobelia groundcover that flowers most of the year. The interior landscape recreates the high desert atmosphere the couple enjoys so much. Here yucca, ocotillo, aloes, cacti, and agaves grow among colorful flowering plants. A variety of euphorbia bears chartreuse flowers in summer. A stand of kangaroo paws contributes brilliant red and yellow flowers in late spring through fall, attracting hummingbirds that dart from flower to flower.

The restrained plant palette and the rhythmic repetition of specific plant groups make the small space seem larger. Each plant has been carefully selected and placed to optimize its relationship and association with surrounding plants. For example, blue agave with black edged fleshy leaves is combined with black aeonium 'Zwartkop' and blue kleinia. The resulting landscape evokes the sense of a Persian carpet, rich in opulent color, form, pattern, and motifs.

A GARDEN OF 1000 PLANTS

ROSAURA ULVESTAD

LAGUNA BEACH

During her first year in Laguna Beach, Rosaura Ulvestad allowed the weeds to flourish while she observed sun and shade patterns in the garden. The second year, she amended the clay soil with gypsum, added some perennial plants, and waited to see how they fared. The third year, she tackled her corner lot with vigor. Now, ten years later, the garden evokes her native Spain, while harmoniously retaining elements of a Laguna Beach cottage garden. Rosaura designed the garden herself, selecting the myriad plants and tending them twice a week. Gardening comes naturally to her, the legacy of her mother and grandmother who were avid gardeners on their Catalonian estate.

This is a plant lover's garden, containing a thousand plants by Rosaura's estimate. The space seems larger because she uses techniques of rhythm and repetition of the same plants throughout the area. Shrubs like lavatera, shrimp plant, Chinese lanterns, and heliotrope give definition and height.

Rosaura planned the space to showcase colorful flowers in every season, flowers that spill over the retaining wall, scramble up arbors and trellises leading from one garden vignette to another, and meander through the seating patios. Among the perennials are various salvias, helichrysum, and cranesbill geraniums. Annuals like amaranth, cleome, and Mexican primrose add splashes of color while forget-me-nots and borage enrich the display by freely reseeding throughout the beds. Rosaura simply removes

them from some spaces and lets them flourish in others. She loves roses, especially the David Austin English roses. Over the years she has included seventy-two different varieties. Some, like 'Mr. Lincoln', soar up to six feet tall. There is also a secret garden where she grows vegetables and herbs.

Rosaura loves to spend time in her garden, especially when she's not engaged in gardening chores. "My garden is my refuge," she says. She shares her passion for gardening and this beautiful space by opening it for local garden tours.

SOFT, PEACEFUL & ROMANTIC

MISSY SCHWEIGER

CORONA DEL MAR

One of Missy Schweiger's early ideas for her garden was to segment the front entry and lawn into two distinct garden rooms linked by a narrow arbor. Planting beds are defined by river rock and birch trees, selected for their shimmering leaves and light bark, and are complemented by the hundred-year-old eucalyptus trees originally on the property.

Within these "bones" or structure, Missy created a green and white garden that is soft, peaceful, and romantic, with ferns and carefully selected flowering plants—foxgloves, hydrangea, salvia—to add splashes of color. She favors plants with old-fashioned form and fragrance. In winter, delicate white and pink camellia blossoms emerge from the deep green, glossy foliage. White calla lilies bloom in spring, replaced in summer by dahlias. Roses rim the perimeter. Her favorite 'Abraham Darby' is an English rose with very fragrant old-fashioned blossoms of soft apricot. She adds flowers according to her mood. Some years fuchsias capture her fancy; other times foxgloves. To the delight of her two-year-old grandson, Missy has included a model railroad that circles the base of a eucalyptus tree. The train complements the garden, evoking an aura of peace and nostalgia.

INDEX